M000116782

© 1993 Happy Books, Milan

This 1994 edition published by Derrydale Books,
distributed by Random House Value Publishing, Inc.,
40 Engelhard Avenue, Avenel, New Jersey 07001

Random House
New York • Toronto • London • Sydney • Auckland
Printed in Italy

MY FIRST BOOK

story by
Vezio Melegari

illustrations by
Giovanni Giannini
Violayne Hulné

DERRYDALE BOOKS
NEW YORK • AVENEL, NEW JERSEY

EVERYONE LOVES THE BEACH!

Isn't it fun to open a book and see a beautiful beach with lots of happy people?

There are the little foxes of the Merry family, who live in the city—Daddy, Mommy, Marky, and Megan.

There are the puppies of the Felicity family, who live in the country. What are their names? Daddy, Mommy, Ophelia, Horatio, and Benny, the smallest of the family.

lifeguard

Megan Merry

beach ball

Mommy Merry

crab

Marky Merry

Daddy Merry

Mommy Allegro

wave

mussel

jellyfish

shell

sea snail

oyster

hermit crab

seahorse

starfish

6

cabins

fishing pole

net

beach umbrella

Captain Allegro

motorboat

Mommy Felicity

Daddy Felicity

beach chair

sand castle

Hillary Allegro

Benny Felicity

pail

Ophelia Felicity

rake

water toy

scuba mask

flippers

Isidore Allegro

raft

Horatio Felicity

There are also the kittens of the Allegro family, who live by the sea not far from the beach. Their names? Captain Allegro, Mommy, Isidore, and Hillary.

THE SEASONS

Summer vacation is almost over. "What a pity!" says
Mommy Allegro. "I do so love the seaside . . ."

seagull

sun

SUMMER

sea

boat

oar

AUTUMN

cloud

rain

tree

fallen leaves

"I prefer the autumn," says Mommy Merry.
"I like the leaves that fall from the trees."

"I like the winter best of all," says Mommy Felicity.
"All the snow . . . and sledding."

WINTER

snowman

sled

snow

"And I like the spring," states Captain Allegro.
"There are new leaves on all the trees, and flowers
spring up in the fields."

SPRING

swallow

leaves

eggs

bird

nest

primrose

bud

In the end they all agree that every season has its own beauty.
But summer is over, and our friends must soon leave for
home.
Captain Allegro has an idea. "What would you say to taking
a trip aboard my fishing boat tomorrow and having a goodbye lunch?"
His proposition is met with various "hurrahs," "greats," and
even a "golly gosh!" from Horatio Felicity, who has a great
passion for happy exclamations.

9

A BOAT RIDE

Our friends are aboard the *Octopus*, Captain Allegro's fishing boat. It's a wonderful boat, with sails and a motor and a radio and radar. It has a wide deck with a pilothouse with the wheel and instruments, and beneath the deck are a cabin with bunks, a hold for storing fish, and a special space for the motor.
A motorized raft with Papa Bear and his son Little Bear roars up alongside the *Octopus*. Our friends give the bears a warm welcome, and Mommy Merry invites them to join the happy lunch being served on the deck. Daddy Felicity takes advantage of the moment to announce, "A few weeks from now we're giving a party on our farm in the country, and you're all invited! It's Benny's birthday!"
Everyone crowds around Benny and asks, "What do you want for your birthday?"
While Benny thinks hard, we can look at the boat and then . . . turn the page!

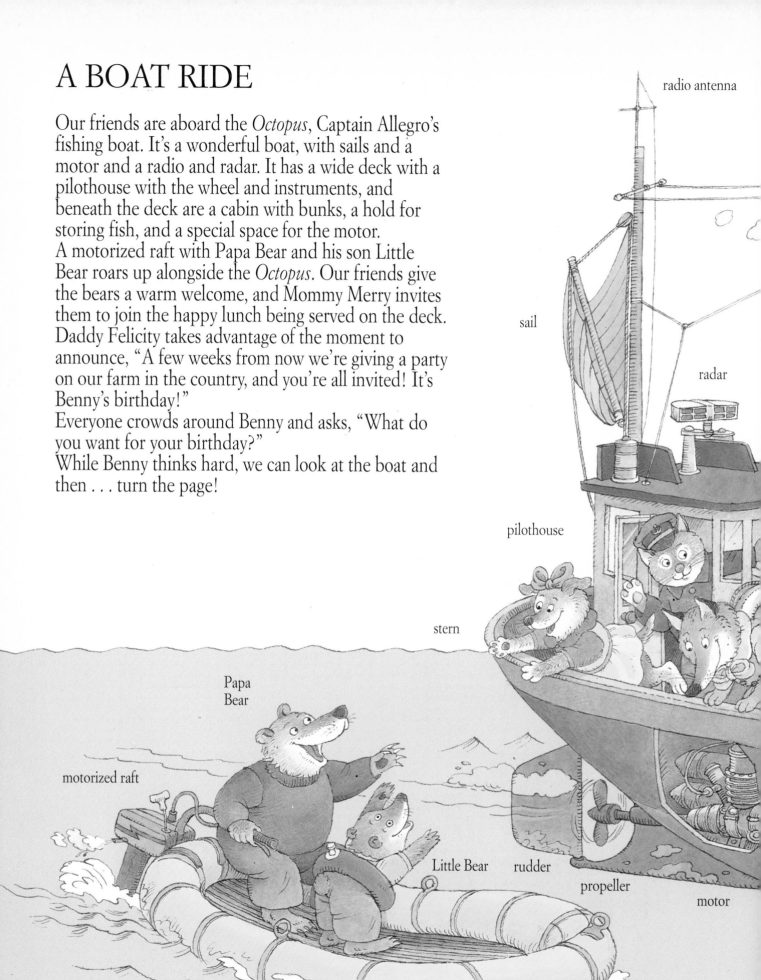

radio antenna

sail

radar

pilothouse

stern

Papa
Bear

motorized raft

Little Bear   rudder

propeller

motor

10

sun

clouds

sail

mast

smokestack

deck

prow

hold for fish

bunks

anchor

T12

11

lightship

telescope

fireboat

coast guard
cutter

rocks

sailboat

lighthouse

fishing boat

LAND AHOY!

Benny is embarrassed because he can't think of
what he wants, but his father comes to his rescue.
"Benny thanks all of you, but I'll tell you what
he'd like. In fact, since this gift comes in various
types, I've decided to make it into a riddle.
What do you say?"
"Hurrah," everyone calls out.
Captain Allegro rings the bell of his fishing
boat and exclaims, "Land ahoy! Look at that
beautiful view!"
Let's take a look too at the wonderful coastline,
with a gulf, lighthouse, island, rocks, and lots
of other boats.

cave

pine wood

river

beach

island

capsized boat

light buoy

reef

divers

submarine

inlet

promontory

wind surfer

aloe

gulf

pebble beach

coast

path

13

AT THE BOTTOM OF THE SEA

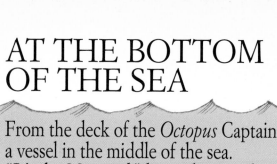

flying fish

From the deck of the *Octopus* Captain Allegro spots a vessel in the middle of the sea.
"It's the *Mermaid*," he exclaims, "the new tourist submarine, and it's about to dive under. It's great. You buy a ticket, get on board, and off you go to take a peek at what's underwater!"
"Really?" "How can they do that?" "How much does it cost?" everyone wants to know.
The captain asks everyone to calm down and stops his fishing boat near the *Mermaid*—and now, if you're good, I'll make it so that everyone, including you, can go aboard the submarine! Everyone ready! Dive!

school of fish

herring

sardine

tourist submarine

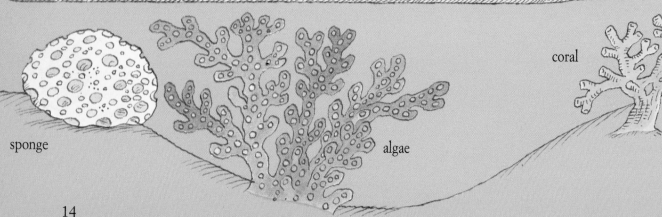

sponge

algae

coral

14

dolphin

seal

whale

sawfish

swordfish

shrimp

cod

tuna

lobster

shark

octopus

squid

hermit crab

sea
anemone

sole

ray

moray eel

A BUSY PORT

Back aboard the *Octopus* after the dive, the group
sets off for port.
"Benny loves music, particularly when it goes
ding ding," says Daddy Felicity, returning to the
subject of Benny's birthday gift.
Marky and Megan call out, "In that case, we should
give him—" but Daddy Felicity interrupts them.
"Not just yet," he says. "I haven't yet asked you
the riddle."
So while you wonder what music that goes *ding ding*
has to do with a present for Benny, let's take a look
at the port. Look how big it is!

merchant
ship

ferry
boat

fishing boat

lighthouse

crane

container

freight train

locomotive

wharf

traffic officer

sailor

crates of fish

delivery van

17

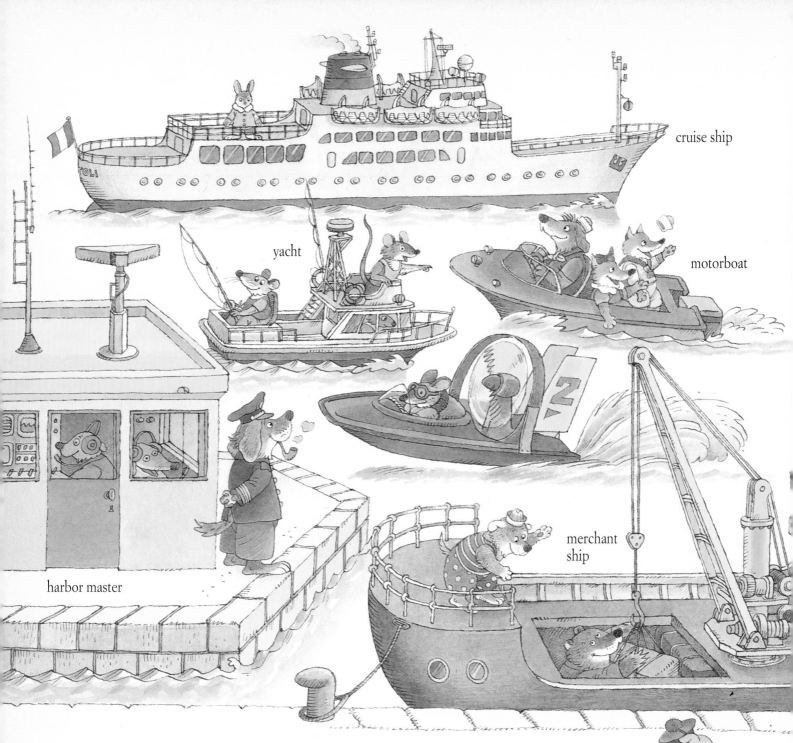

cruise ship

yacht

motorboat

merchant ship

harbor master

SO MANY SHIPS!

Permission is needed to go in and out of the port and to anchor in it. If Captain Allegro has pulled into a dock it means he has permission from the harbor master.

Captain Allegro exclaims, "We shouldn't leave the port without first looking at all the ships. There are cruise ships, tankers, merchant ships . . ."

And we can quietly tag along with all of them.

sailor

oil tanker

tug boat

warehouse

crane

27 A

goods

forklift

pallet

19

lemon
tree

succulent

pineapple

lilac

orchid

A VISIT TO A GREENHOUSE

The Allegro, Merry, and Felicity families are back on
dry land. Is the trip over? Not at all!
The travelers climb aboard a bus, and the captain
announces, "Before going home, there's something
else you should see that may come as a surprise.
I'm going to show you that along the coastline there
are many kinds of fruit and flowers!"
The bus stops after a short ride, and our friends
get out and enter a big greenhouse. The greenhouse
is a place made specially for the cultivation of flowers
and plants that need someplace indoors and
protected to grow.
How many plants and flowers can you name?

mimosa

carnation

20

banana

palm

orange tree

lily

gardener

jasmine

daisy

tulip

dahlia

cactus

rose

21

IN THE UNDERBRUSH

Daddy Felicity takes off along a path.
Everyone follows him.
"Let's get back to the subject of the birthday gift,"
he says and takes two coins from his pocket.
"Who can make a triangle with these two coins?"
he asks.
"You need three coins to make a triangle," says
Captain Allegro, arranging three coins on the ground.
"Really?" says Daddy Felicity. "Even so . . ."

path

butterfly

snail

strawberry

foxglove

bee

lily of the valley

fern

honeysuckle

hedgehog

moss

trunk

22

raspberries

ivy

dog
rose

chestnuts

hazelnuts

mushroom

whortleberry

nightingale

fallen
leaves

cuckoo

poisonous
mushroom

stones

He holds the two coins between his thumb and index
finger and uses them to draw a triangle in the sand!
"Hurrah!" exclaims Isidore. "I know what the
present for Benny is!"
Have you understood too? While you give it some
thought, let's take a look around the underbrush,
all the plants and bushes that grow beneath the trees.
Some of them have fruit that is good to eat.
Do you recognize them?

triangle

violet

AROUND THE LAKE

The group arrives at a lake.
"Speaking of lakes," says Daddy Felicity. "Who can tell me what—"
But Horatio interrupts him, saying, "Oh, Daddy, please, that's enough! Everywhere we go there are riddles! What does the trick with the triangle have to do with the gift for Benny?"
"Oh, you'll see soon enough," says Daddy Felicity. "In fact, I'll guide you to the gift by way of a contest!"

ducks

dragonflies

frog

cattails

boat

lake

toad

water snake

trout

pike

perch

turtle

eel

24

"Hurrah!" all the children yell in chorus. "Let's do it!"
"But really," protests Mommy Merry. "There are so many contests on television, although those are game shows with prizes."
"There's never been a prize like this one," says Daddy Felicity. But listen! While they talk about prizes, let's stay calm and discover the life that thrives in the lake: frogs, tadpoles, toads, and birds, aquatic plants and flowers, and fish, lots of kinds of fish . . .

butterfly

stepping-stones

stream

kingfisher

fishing pole

frog

dock

waterlily

tadpoles

carp

catfish

snail

25

spaghetti

rice

kitchen

ham

pots

meat

roast chicken

stove

oven

refrigerator

lettuce

pan

oil

vinegar

potatoes

carrot

salt

cook

sausage

pepper

cook

tomatoes

corn

salami

milk

rolling pin and dough

mixer

strainer

flour

measuring cup

cream

eggs

butter

26

menu

glass

THE RESTAURANT CONTEST

Later on, in a restaurant, Daddy Felicity explains his contest. "What Benny really wants is something that resembles several other things. For example, when migratory birds fly they form something. Another thing is a pretty shape, one of those you study in school. Another is something you can find in the tool boxes of carpenters and plumbers. And then there's something way up in the sky that is well known to people who learn astronomy. But you can't forget that Benny likes music that goes *ding ding*. Enough?"

plate

spoon

napkin

fruit

turkey

cheese

waitress

salad

cake

ice cream

French fries

bread

sugar

spaghetti

water

coffee

roof

pigeon

children's room

books

beds

bedroom

bed

bathroom

stairs

kitchen

mat

blackbird

28

THE MERRY HOME

chimney

antenna

window

robin

dove

patio

Summer vacation is over. The Merry family and the Felicitys have gone home: the Merrys live in the city, and the Felicitys in the country. The Allegro family has gone to their home in a town by the sea.

Here we are in the home of the Merrys. They are truly neat and tidy. With a family like that, everything is in its place: the refrigerator is in the kitchen, the television in the living room, the beds in the bedrooms. All their books are on shelves, and their cassettes and VCR are in special places. Daddy, Mommy, Marky, and Megan are talking about Daddy Felicity's contest. All of a sudden, Mommy exclaims, "I have an idea. Tomorrow, when I go to the market . . ."

television and video cassette recorder

cassettes

living room

crane

A CONSTRUCTION SITE

The next day Mommy Merry goes shopping. She has a plan in mind, and she goes to a construction site near her house. She stops to look at the bulldozer and the steam shovel, the cement mixer, and the crane.
I'll bet that you, too, are interested, and you probably have a great time watching machines at work.

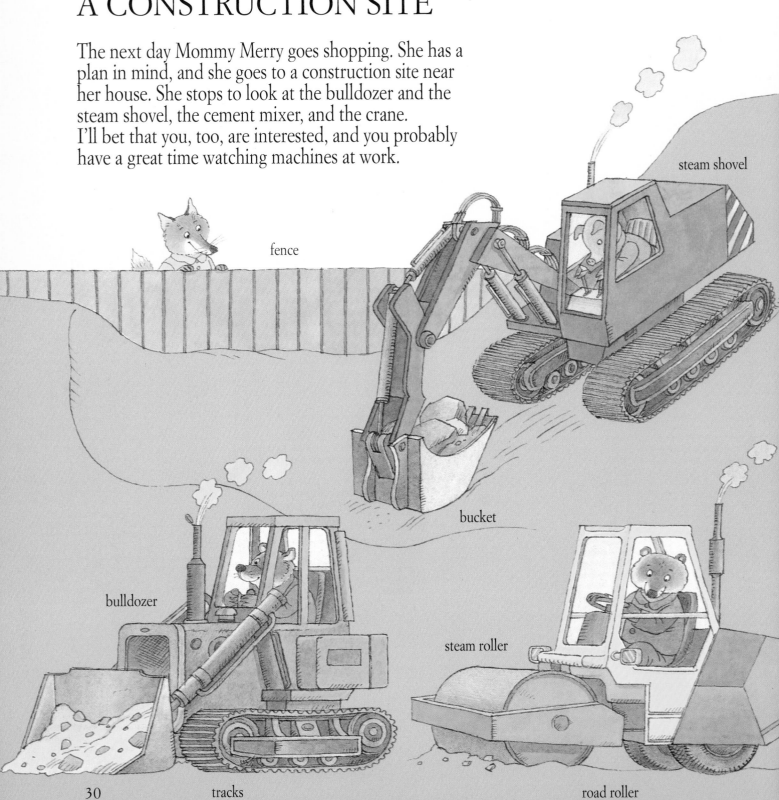

steam shovel

fence

bucket

bulldozer

steam roller

30   tracks   road roller

crane operator

pneumatic drill

helmet

worker

cement mixer

31

BUILDING A HOUSE

Mommy Merry's plan is to speak with Manlius, a plumber friend of hers who works together with plasterers, carpenters, electricians, painters, and other skilled workers building new houses. And while you look around the house being built, I'll pay attention to what Mommy Merry asks Manlius the plumber.

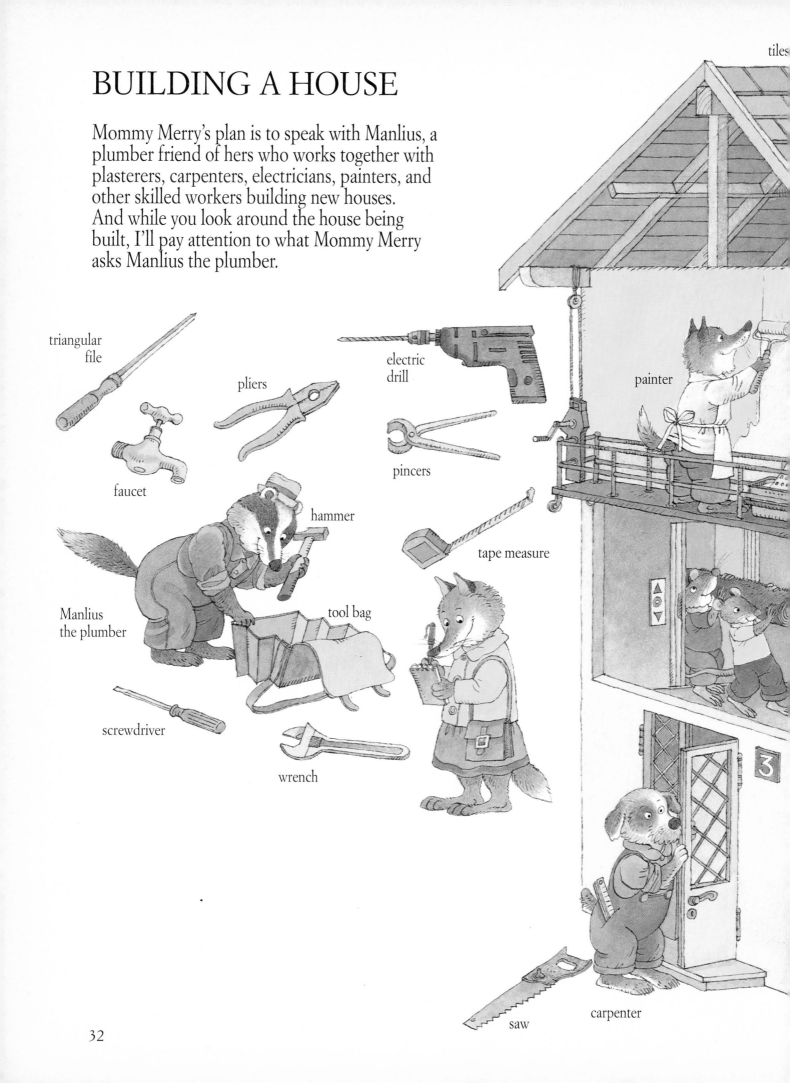

triangular file

faucet

pliers

electric drill

pincers

hammer

tape measure

Manlius the plumber

tool bag

screwdriver

wrench

painter

tiles

3

carpenter

saw

roof

carpenter

mason

fireplace

bricks

plasterer

radiator

stairs

electrician

caretaker

hedge

ice cream wagon

sand box

balloon

baby carriage

monkey bars

slide

fountain

swing

pond

34

monument

trees

ring-around-the-rosy

jump rope

skateboard

roller skates

bicycle

path

flowers

flower bed

IN THE PARK

Mommy Merry arrives at the park.
There are lots of children busy playing. But she does not
have the time to watch them. She sits down and takes
out of her purse her notepad with the notes she took
from Manlius the plumber. She reads the notes, thinks
a while, and then shakes her head.
"Contest or no contest," she says to herself, "I'll decide
what present to give Benny only after I see the toy
departments in the big department stores. After all,
Benny is young and would almost certainly like almost
any toy, as long as it's interesting."
She stands up and walks away, as curious as ever.

bench

sparrows

35

THE DEPARTMENT STORE

Here is Mommy Merry in the big department store, trying to make up her mind in the middle of cars, blocks, trains, and other wonders.

"Excuse me," she says to a sales clerk. "In your opinion, what can a little boy who is six or seven years old do with a triangular file, a hammer, a wrench, and other similar items?"

"Take a house apart," says the sales clerk, smiling.

"But Benny is not a bad boy," says Mommy Merry.

"Well then," responds the sales clerk. "He can become a passionate 'do-it-yourselfer.'"

"A what-do-you-say?"

"He could do woodwork, for example. He could make little things out of plywood. He could make pen holders or picture frames or shelves." Saying this, the sales clerk shows her a handsome little tool kit with lots of tools just like those used by Manlius, only smaller and, of course, brand new.

"Wrap it up for me, please," exclaims Mommy Merry. "I've found it!"

clothing department

clothing department

"do-it-yourself" tool kit

sweaters

cap

jacket

pants

try-on room

sales clerk

shopper

blocks

doll

car

train

toy department

escalator

window display

mannequins

hat

perfumes

dress

mannequins

skirt

glove

GETTING AROUND IN THE CITY

The big city offers many means of transportation:
trolleys, trolley-buses, buses, taxis. These are called
surface transportation. And for under the ground?
There is the subway, which runs on tracks beneath
the city.
If you've never seen a subway, you can do so now,
following Mommy Merry who, a little tired but happy,
is going home by subway.
Let's listen to her talking to the woman sitting next to
her. "Have you ever heard of 'do-it-yourself'?" she asks,
but the conversation ends there, because the subway is
fast, and Mommy Merry must get off already.

taxi

newspaper stand

escalator

token booth

subway map

seats

wastebasket

subway

trolley

trolley-bus

bus

subway entrance

street

bus stop

tunnel

train

stairs

poster

driver

passageway

platform

passengers

DOWNTOWN

Meanwhile, Daddy Merry is at work downtown
in the city center, the oldest part of the city.
In that area are the city hall, museum, library,
and the most elegant stores and restaurants.

museum

restaurant

telephone
booth

movie theater

drain

ice cream
store

bakery

coffee shop

sidewalk

barber shop

40

library

church

pedestrians

delivery wagon

police officer

traffic light

city hall

monument

pedestrian crossing

dance school

bookstore

pharmacy

post office

letter carrier

41

garage

cashier

gas pumps

race car

roller skates

Manlius's plumbing van

dump truck

station wagon

car

motor scooter

A TRIP TO THE CITY

"Have a very good day all day," says Horatio Felicity, as he rushes into Daddy Merry's bookstore.
"What a pleasant surprise!" exclaims the bookseller.
"But what is a Felicity doing here, so far from the family farm?"
"I came into the city on a school trip, so I have to

car wash

mechanic

van

school bus

police car

garbage
collectors

leave right away, but my parents say hello and
wish you good luck for the contest."
"I think I'm on the right track," says Daddy
Merry. "In fact, you know what I'm going to do?"
But Horatio has already left. And you know what
we'll do? Let's follow Horatio's school bus.
That way we can see more of the vehicles used in
the streets of the city.

PIZZA

27
A°

books

window display

photocopier

book of
fairy tales

pop-up
book

calculator

loose-leaf
book

telepho

IN THE BOOKSTORE

While Daddy Merry is busy, let's look around his shop.
Look at all the books! Books for adults and books for
children. There are pop-up books and books of fairy
tales, big books and very small books. And on so many
subjects! Look! There's a book all about shapes!
Daddy Merry flips through it, looks through it again,
and then suddenly rushes to the telephone.
"Hello? Hi, it's Merry here. How are you, Felicity? I
just saw Horatio. . . . No, he didn't tell me anything.
But I have something to say to you. When you
described the contest, you said something about a
pretty shape, like those you learn in school. I don't
suppose you were talking about—."
But the roar of a passing motorcycle fills the bookstore
so we can't hear the last word.
"That's it, right?" continues Daddy Merry. "You don't
want to tell me? You're right, it would be unfair to the
others if you told me. We'll play by the rules. Thanks!
Goodbye and greetings to the entire family."

AN OFFICE IN THE COUNTRY

Bleep! Bleep! Bleep! The telephone in Daddy Felicity's office certainly makes a strange sound. *Bleep! Bleep! Bleep!* goes the machine, and out of it comes a page of paper. This is the fax machine, a new invention that transmits words or pictures instead of voices. There it is in the middle of the tables, shelves, and cabinets in the office that Daddy Felicity has on his farm. He looks at the long page of paper and reads: "Dear friend, are you sure we have to spend a night studying the stars in order to find out what Benny wants for his birthday? It's a nice thing to do, but it's beginning to get chilly, and the sky isn't always clear. Greetings, Captain Allegro and family."

Daddy Felicity laughs. Then he types something on a piece of paper, inserts it in his fax machine, dials a telephone number, and the fax—*Bleep! Bleep! Bleep!*—sends his response. What did he write?

receiving a fax

typewriter

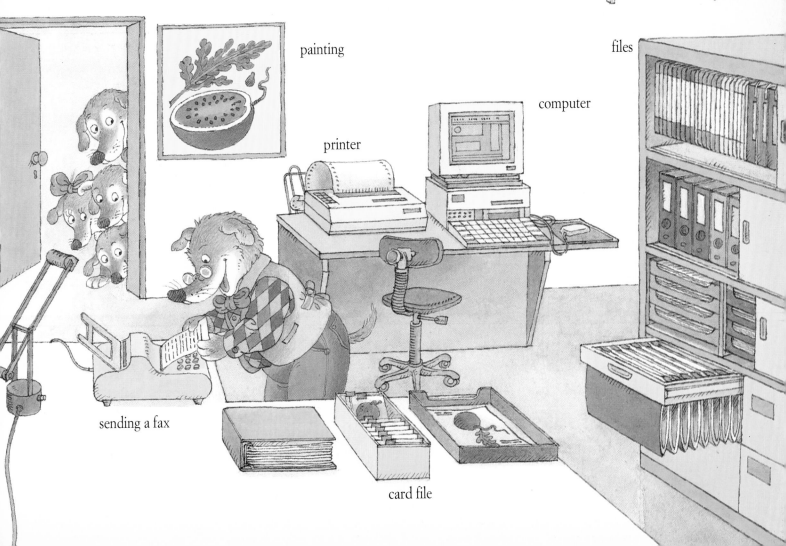

painting

files

computer

printer

sending a fax

card file

fishing boat

thermometer

barometer

telephone

filing cabinet

fax

telescope

telephone directory

envelopes

ship in a bottle

desk calendar

fountain pen

rocking chair

nautical chart

radio

compass

binoculars

notepad

46

fishing pole

clock

wall calendar

fishing net

cap

raincoat

fish trap

rope

AN OFFICE BY THE SEA

To find out about Daddy Felicity's response to Captain Allegro, we have to go to the captain's office, which is in a building overlooking the port where the Octopus is docked. The office certainly has unusual furnishings! More than an office, it seems like a storeroom for sailor's gear!

Coming out of Captain Allegro's fax machine is a page with the message sent by Daddy Felicity. "Look at the stars, in particular look for a constellation composed of only three stars . . . but don't forget that Benny likes music that goes *ding ding*!"

Captain Allegro reads the fax and sighs. "This contest is complicated. What we need is a family meeting."

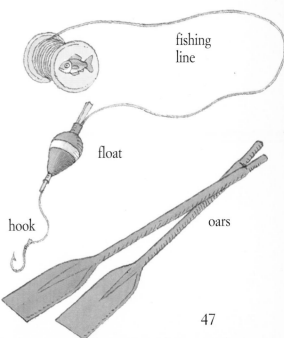

fishing line

float

hook

oars

47

Pluto

Neptune

Uranus

Saturn

star

satellite

astronaut

spaceship

lunar vehicle

meteorite

moon

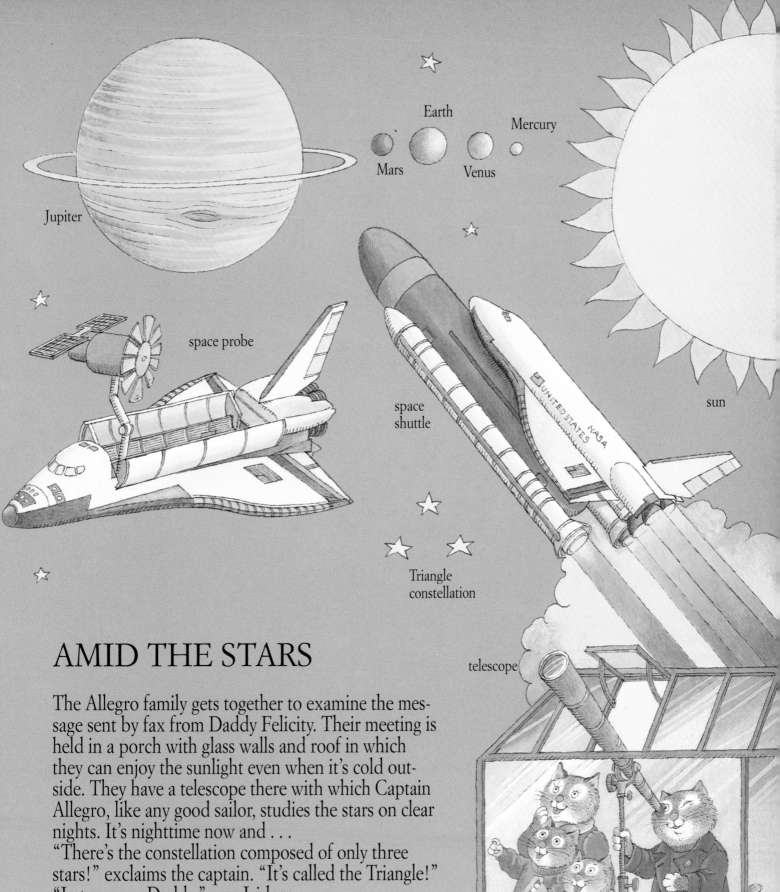

Jupiter

Earth

Mars

Venus

Mercury

sun

space probe

space
shuttle

Triangle
constellation

telescope

AMID THE STARS

The Allegro family gets together to examine the message sent by fax from Daddy Felicity. Their meeting is held in a porch with glass walls and roof in which they can enjoy the sunlight even when it's cold outside. They have a telescope there with which Captain Allegro, like any good sailor, studies the stars on clear nights. It's nighttime now and . . .

"There's the constellation composed of only three stars!" exclaims the captain. "It's called the Triangle!"

"Let me see, Daddy," says Isidore.

"Certainly not," says Mommy Allegro. "Let's close the window. It's too cold at night!"

"Wait a minute," says Hillary. "I think I understand."

THE JOY OF FLYING

Do you think Hillary is about to solve the contest?
To find out, we have to follow her while she visits her
friend Natasha. They both love flying and hope to
become pilots!
"I want to go way up immediately," says Hillary.
"Why such a hurry?" asks Natasha.
"I'll go out in space and grab three stars for Benny,"
explains Hillary.
"Oh, what a romantic you are," exclaims Natasha. And
while the two friends are laughing, let's take a leap into
the air and look around among the clouds.

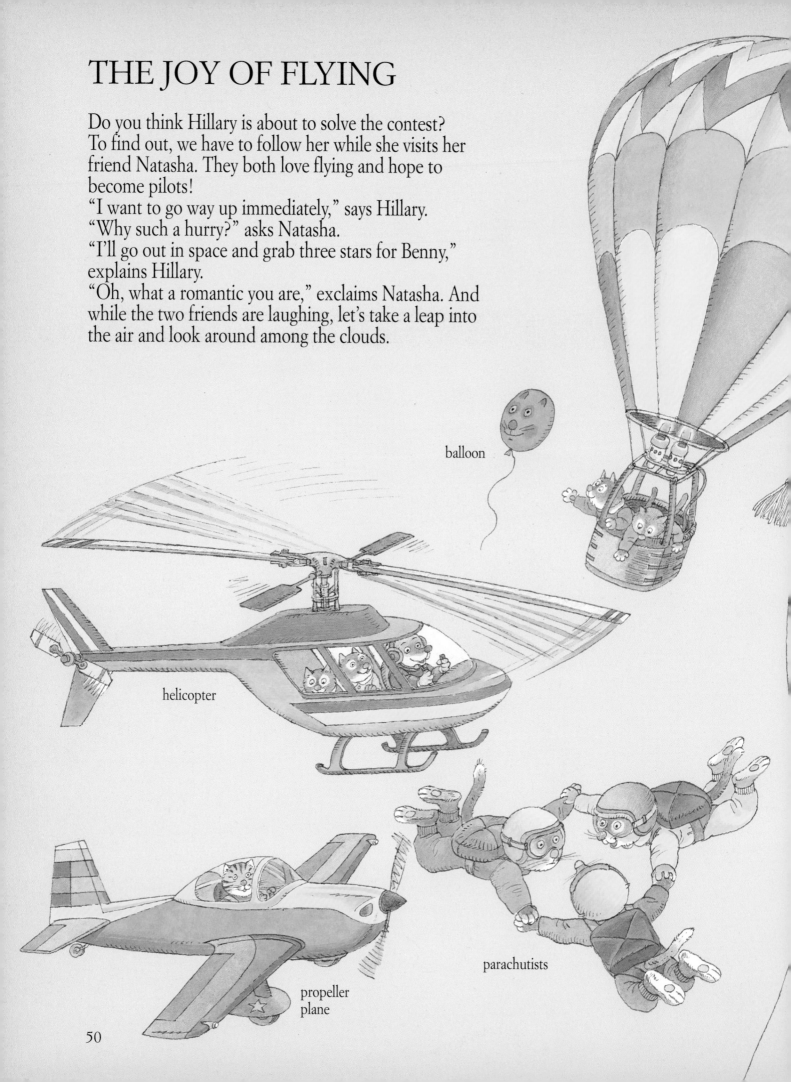

balloon

helicopter

parachutists

propeller
plane

50

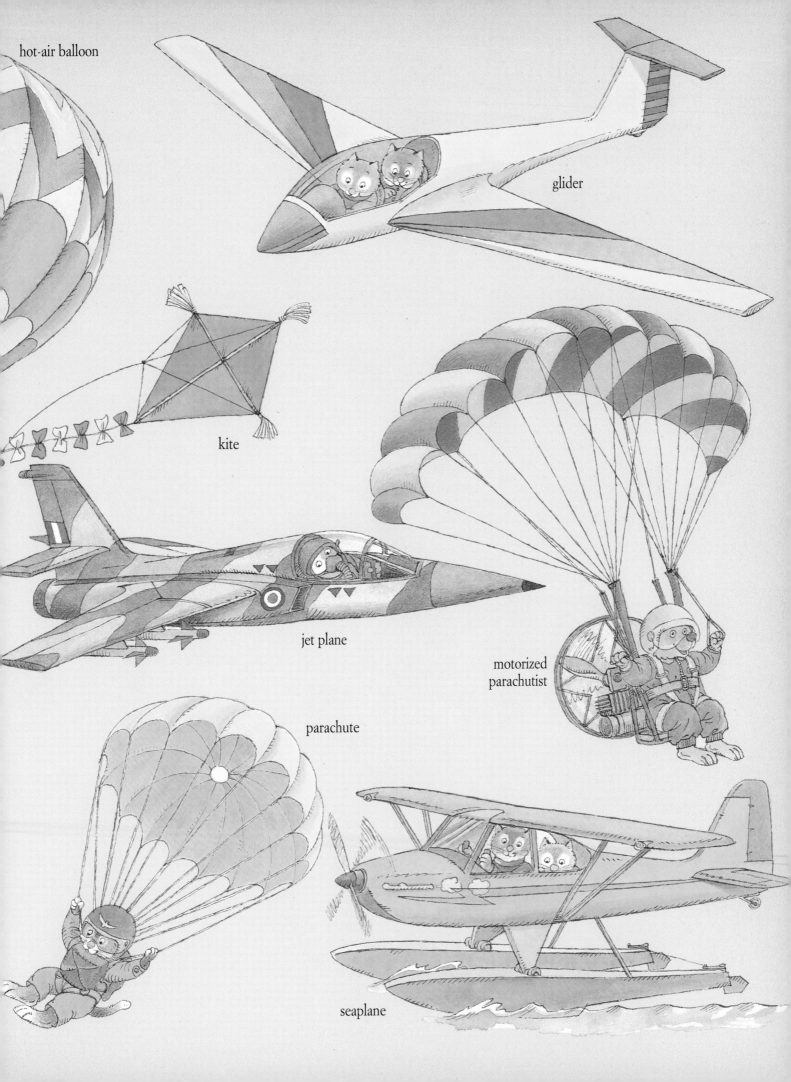

hot-air balloon

glider

kite

jet plane

motorized parachutist

parachute

seaplane

canned goods

mineral water

detergents

eggs

shopper

cheeses

salamis

basket

scale

pineapple   pears   plums

grapes   strawberries   bananas   grapefruit

52

AT THE SUPERMARKET

What are Hillary and Isidore doing at the supermarket? Are they there to find the solution to Daddy Felicity's contest? Or are they just trying to confuse us? But what can they be hoping to find at the supermarket, amid peppers, frozen foods, and detergents? Actually, it's none of this. The two have simply obeyed their mother's request to accompany her on her shopping rounds. And while they load their cart full of every kind of product, we can follow the shoppers one at a time up and down the aisles to investigate the store. Let's see who reaches the check-out counter first. But don't forget to get your receipt!

yogurt   milk

margarine   butter

puddings   fruit juices

chocolate

pepper

cart

butter

bag

change purse

shopping cart

mustard

check-out counter

cashier

bread

sardines

eggs

bottles

53

THE FORTUNE-TELLER

Let's follow Mommy Allegro as she examines what's on sale at the open-air market held in her neighborhood every week. Lots of things! Fruit, vegetables, flowers, candy, toys, pots and pans, and linens. There's even a fortune-teller! "A fortune-teller! Just what I need to solve the contest!" exclaims Mommy Allegro and immediately tells the fortune-teller her problem. The fortune-teller looks into her crystal ball. "I see . . . I see a flock of birds in flight. I see . . . I see a constellation of three stars! I see . . . I see a geometric shape! That will be five dollars, please."
"Oh!" exclaims Mommy Allegro. She pays and returns to examining the wares, slowly thinking about the mysterious clues.

florist

chrysanthemum

zinnia

pansy

bouquet of flowers

scale

squash

lettuce

turnips

shopper

cucumbers   corn   eggplants   carrots   string beans

housewares

pans

pot

linens

T-shirt

dress

pillow cases

sheets

teapot

frying pan

ladle

bagpipe

toys

slippers

jogging suit

fortune-teller

candy

55

TENSION IN THE MELON PATCH

Brring! Brring! rings the portable telephone of the Felicity Perfect Melons Company. It's Mommy Felicity's personal phone, and she's in the melon patch measuring a truly enormous specimen. She takes her measuring tape in one hand and holds the phone to her ear with the other. But first she rests her chin on the melon to hold it steady.

stones

grass

hoe

shovel

stake

string

furrow

hoe

seeds

furrow

rake

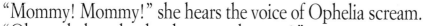

watering can

"Mommy! Mommy!" she hears the voice of Ophelia scream.
"Oh, my baby, what has happened to you?"
"Oh, Mommy, if only you knew!" screams Ophelia into the phone.
"What's wrong? Are you hurt?"
"No, I'm fine. I've discovered what present to give Benny. That way Daddy can save a hundred pounds of watermelons!"

buds

pear tree

apple tree

ladder

crates

water pump

hose

three-wheeled van

portable telephone

Mommy Felicity sighs and relaxes—a little too much!
The watermelon slips away from under her chin.
In order to catch it she drops the phone, bringing the
conversation to a sudden end and keeping us from hear-
ing Ophelia's idea. At least for now. But don't lose heart.
Instead, enjoy the garden.

pitchfork

watermelon

eggplant

melon

squash

strawberry

basket

wheelbarrow

57

kettledrums

triangle

cymbals

bass drum

drum

drummer

BENNY'S ROOM

I know you want to catch up with Ophelia to see what she has discovered. We can't because we don't know where she called from. Why don't we take a close look at Benny's room and his hobbies? We may stumble on the answer.

violin

cello

bassoon

piano

harmonica

recorder

horn

flute

saxophone

clarinet

fife

harp

tuba

orchestra conductor

accordion

bass

trombone

trumpet

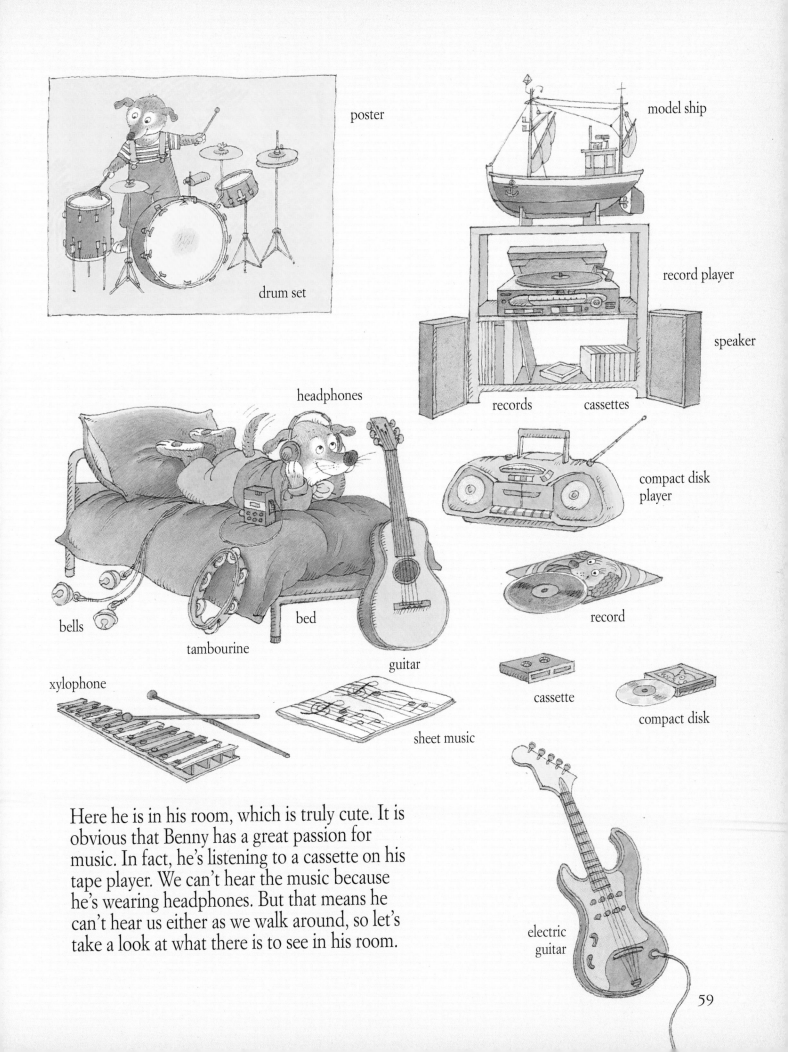

poster

model ship

drum set

record player

speaker

headphones

records   cassettes

compact disk player

bells

bed

record

tambourine

guitar

cassette

compact disk

xylophone

sheet music

Here he is in his room, which is truly cute. It is obvious that Benny has a great passion for music. In fact, he's listening to a cassette on his tape player. We can't hear the music because he's wearing headphones. But that means he can't hear us either as we walk around, so let's take a look at what there is to see in his room.

electric guitar

59

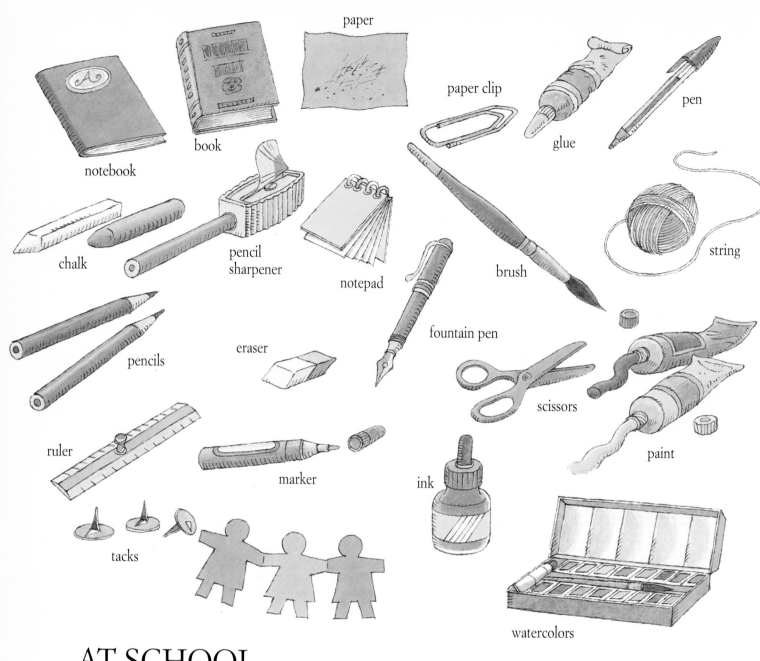

paper

paper clip

glue

pen

book

notebook

chalk

pencil sharpener

notepad

brush

string

pencils

eraser

fountain pen

scissors

paint

ruler

marker

ink

tacks

watercolors

AT SCHOOL

Our visit to Benny's room did not reveal much, but
let's not be discouraged. Now let's follow him to
school and see him talk with his school friends.
"It will be my birthday in a few days," he says.
"You'll probably get lots of great presents," says a friend.
"All of them have promised me one present."
"Only one present?" asks his friend in wonder.
"Yes, but a present from so many people together will
have to be wonderful and important," says Benny.
Can it be that the only way to find out what Benny
wants is to wait until the end of this story?

clothes hooks

video

clock

calendar

rhombus

rectangle

square

circle

teacher

bell

triangle

blackboard

book

desk

stapler

wastebasket

stool

table

square

paper

eraser

chair

61

hay loft

stall

cow

horse

sheep

tractor

goat

trailer

chicken coop

goose

eggs

rabbit

chicks

hen

62

van

crates

VACATION ON THE FARM

"Good day to you!" exclaims a distinguished gentleman who has just arrived at the Felicity farm. "I am Mr. Wolfie."
"Good day!" responds Mommy Felicity.
"Well, then," says the gentleman, "shall we prepare the contract? As I explained on the phone, if you will make your farm available to my tourist agency, we'll transform it into a wonderful vacation spot!"
"To tell you the truth," says Mommy Felicity, "we really haven't given it much thought."
So while she thinks about it, let's walk around the farm.

rooster

pig

waterfall

mill

stream

river

swan

64

ALONG THE RIVER

Daddy Felicity and Mr. Wolfie go out to the river. "The countryside is an ideal place for tourism. It is a new way of spending vacations in contact with nature," explains Mr. Wolfie. "Here's how it works. The tourists, usually people from the city, go to a travel agency and ask for a list of farms that offer rooms for tourists. They choose, pay, and go on vacation in the country. Great idea, don't you think?"

"Goodness!" responds Daddy Felicity. "That means that those of us who live on farms are always on vacation! Thanks for the offer, but right now I haven't got time for tourists. In fact, we're busy organizing the birthday party for our Benny!"

weeping willow

bridge

barge

FIREFIGHTERS

After saying goodbye to Mr. Wolfie, Daddy Felicity
calls Horatio and Ophelia and says, "Let's go see
Grandfather. We have to invite him to Benny's party!"
"Hurrah! Hurrah!" shout the children, jumping for joy.
Why so much happiness? The children love their
grandfather, naturally, but also Grandfather Felicity
is a special grandfather. In fact, he's the captain of a
fire brigade.
The brigade's firehouse is a wonderful place: there
are pumper trucks, hook-and-ladder trucks, oxygen
tanks, and fire extinguishers.
"Grandfather, can I get in the pump truck?"
asks Horatio, climbing in.
"Grandfather, what should I give Benny?" asks
Ophelia.
"It's a secret, but I don't see why I can't tell you.
Your grandmother and I are going to give him—."
But in that moment Horatio turns on the siren, and
we can't hear what Grandfather says!

pump truck

ladder

fire extinguisher

siren

helmet

firefighter

hook-and-ladder truck

WHO'S AT HOME IN A CASTLE?

"Today we're taking a trip," says Daddy Felicity to his family. "We're going to the old castle!"
A chorus of hurrahs rises from the three children Horatio, Ophelia, and Benny.
"Let's go," says Daddy Felicity. "Of all the buildings you can see in a landscape, the castle is always the one that stands out the most, because castles are always built on an elevated spot and have high towers."
"Why is that?" asks Ophelia.
"Because being high makes it easier to defend. The people from all around would take refuge in the castle when an enemy army was nearby."
"Is it true that there are ghosts in old castles?" asks Ophelia.
"Oh, my," says Mommy Felicity, almost breathless after the climb. "Castles are inhabited by lizards, memories"—a strange creaking sound interrupts her—"and, for those who believe, by ghosts!"

lance

battlement

wall   sentry

helmet

knight

drawbridge

foot soldiers

page

tower

banner

queen throne

king

throne room

minstrel

armor

trumpeters

Ferris
wheel

balloons

clown

AT THE AMUSEMENT PARK

Time passes quickly. As Benny's birthday draws near,
some of the guests begin their journey. The Allegro family
leaves the *Octopus* at anchor and goes by car toward the
Felicity Perfect Melons Company.
"Anyone want to stop at the amusement park?" asks
Captain Allegro, who lets Mommy Allegro drive since
he's used to the fishing boat's big wheel.
"Yesssss!" answer Isidore and Hillary together.
Evidently, they're no longer worried about the question
of what to give Benny. Perhaps they hope to find something in the amusement park. Let's follow them on the
merry-go-round—and have fun!

cotton
candy

lollipop

candy
apple

70

roller
coaster

cashier

merry-go-round

UP IN THE MOUNTAINS

To reach the Felicity family the Allegros must pass over mountains. In fact, after stopping at the amusement park, they drive onto a superhighway. By way of bridges, overpasses, and tunnels, the superhighway travels across the mountains and then leads down toward the plain where the Felicity family lives. Mommy Allegro looks at the distant peaks covered in snow and admires the hills and the skiers.
"I'd like to learn how to ski some day," she says.
"We would too!" shouts the rest of the family.
"Well, then, we'll look into it on the way back," says the captain.
And you? Which do you prefer, skiing or sledding?

chair-lift

cable car

mountains

ski slope

skier

gates

skis

sled

72

ge

fir tree

snow

poles

ski lift

73

ambulance

tractor-trailer
truck

bus

trailer

tow truck

THE SERVICE STATION

The trip on the superhighway continues.
"Service stations have not only gas pumps but also
snack bars, cafeterias, and restaurants," says
Mommy Allegro.
"They must have lots of good things," sighs Hillary.
"And you can eat them right there," agrees Isidore.
"Okay, I've understood," says the captain. "You're
hungry and you want to stop at the nearest cafeteria."
"Good idea," says Mommy Allegro. "We can buy
a newspaper and get a full tank of gas."
"And put something tasty in our tummies,"
concludes Hillary.
Can you really do such things on a superhighway?
Sure you can. It's a lot of fun.

service station

toilet

74

PETROL

truck

gas pump

station attendant

motorcycle

BAR

parking

car

7

75

THE RAILROAD STATION

Look at this: it's the Merry family! They seem to have decided to travel to the Felicity farm by train—that's why they're arriving at the station with all those bags.

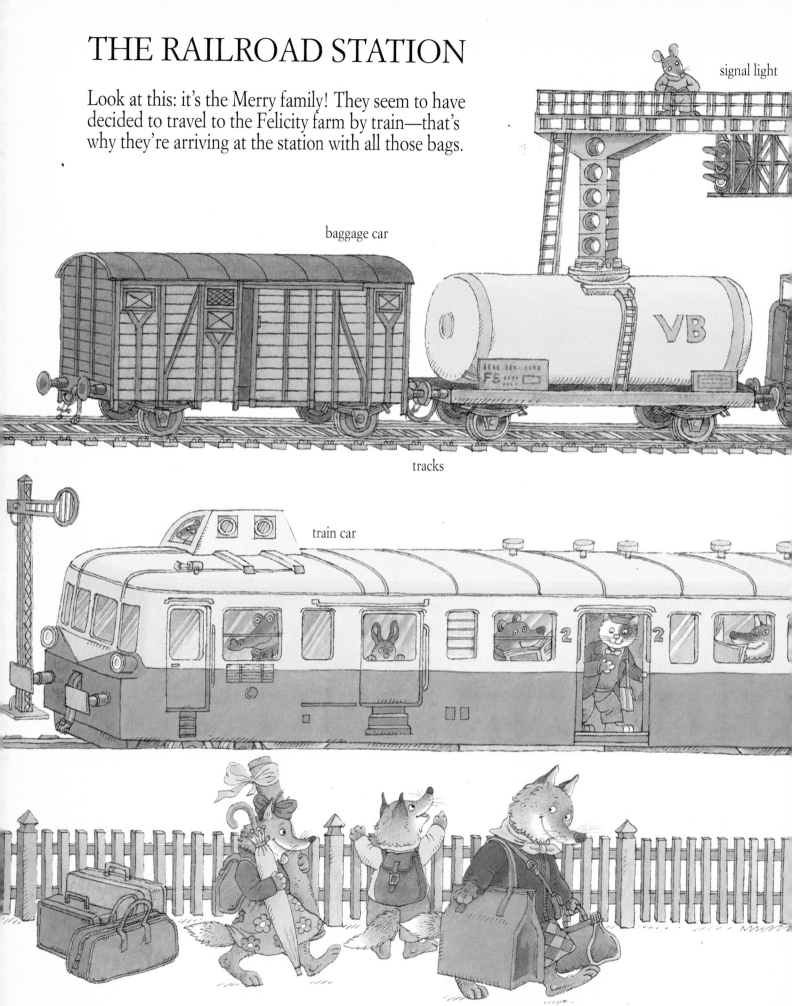

signal light

baggage car

tracks

train car

But they aren't all there! Daddy Merry is missing! Where could he be? Is he off somewhere trying to solve the famous contest? Let me know if you spot him. Meanwhile, we'll get out of the way for Mommy Merry, Megan, and Marky.

coal tender

steam
locomotive

schedule

clock

waiting room

ticket counter

train yard

rail car

tracks

platform

travelers   window   seats   conductor   baggage

suitcases

78

ALL ABOARD!

Waiting to get on the train, the family has time to investigate the enormous station.
Marky says, "I'd like to know how many kinds of cars a train can have."
Megan says, "I'd like to know why the station master has that round sign and the whistle."
And Mommy Merry sighs, "I'd like to know why your father isn't here to help us with these bags."

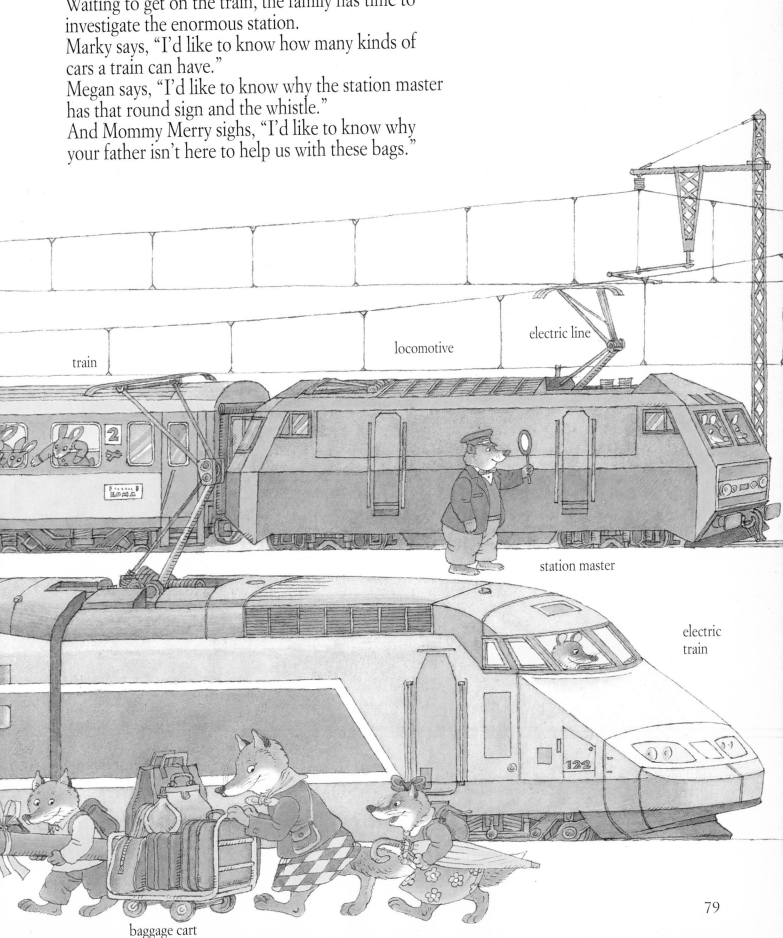

train

locomotive

electric line

station master

electric train

baggage cart

79

IN THE GRAND HOTEL

What is Daddy Merry up to? Why is he not with his family? Why is he asking for a room in the Grand Hotel? Has he found the answer to the contest? In the lobby of the hotel Daddy Merry says to the desk clerk, "Wake me up early tomorrow morning, please."

The desk clerk is the most important person in the hotel. He takes care of the guests. He calls taxis for them, purchases train tickets for them, makes their theater reservations, handles their phone calls, takes care of their baggage and has it brought to their rooms. He oversees the elevators, watches over the keys to the rooms, and, as you've just learned, wakes guests up on time if they ask. Finally, the desk clerk has to answer questions like this: "What do you know about triangles?"

Now who could have asked him that?

luggage

room

maid

elevator

keys

mailboxes

porter

bell

desk clerk

81

toilet

seat

flap

wing

windows

airplane

cockpit

stewardess

aisle

baggage

jet engine

A PLANE TRIP

This is why Daddy Merry wanted to be awakened
early. He had to take an early airplane to get home.
His mission is accomplished!
What does that mean? To find out we have to wait
for the plane to land. Let's use the time to enjoy the
trip, examine the airplane, and have fun looking at
the passengers.

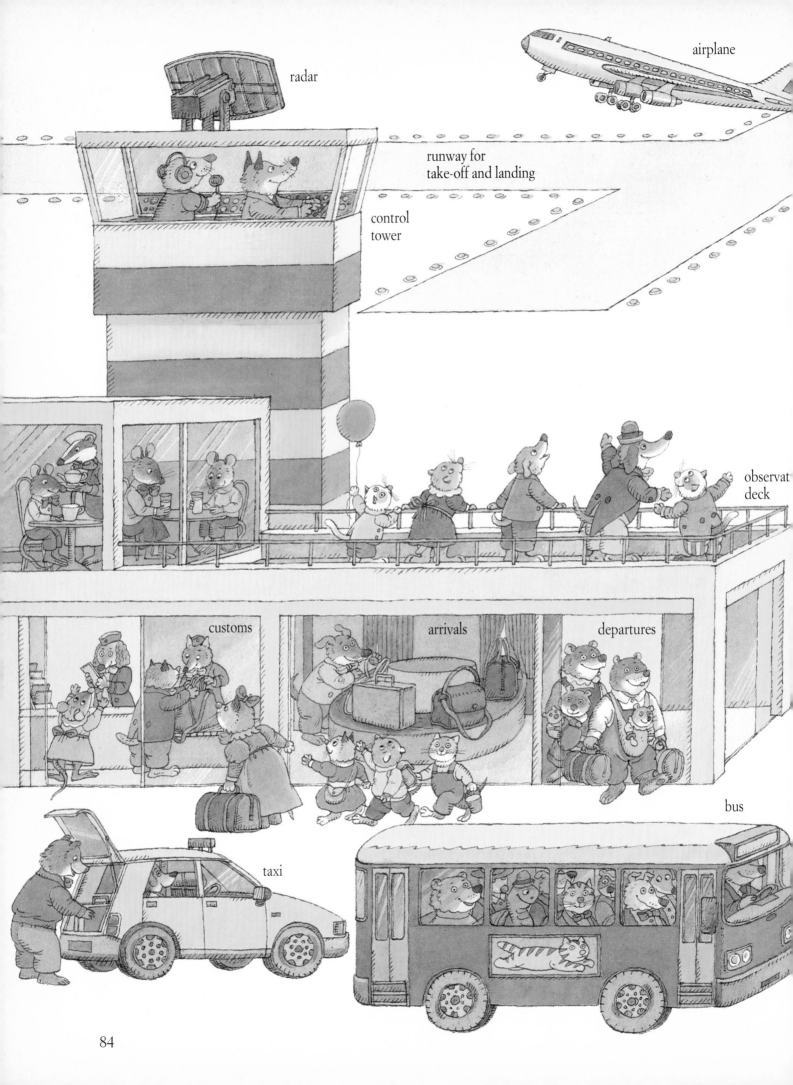

radar

airplane

runway for
take-off and landing

control
tower

observat
deck

customs

arrivals

departures

bus

taxi

hangars

boarding
ramp

bus

baggage carts

AT THE AIRPORT

Here we are at the airport! The airplane has just land-
ed with the passengers and their luggage.
Daddy Merry makes his way out the exit with his suit-
case. He finds a telephone booth, dials a number,
hangs up, then dials the number again . . . It's clear he
can't get through. But he doesn't seem worried.
He goes back toward the exit and gets in a taxi, which
takes off and disappears in the traffic!
We can only look around in wonder and observe how
big and lively the airport is.

telephone

BIRTHDAY BATHS

In the Felicity home the three children are taking baths to make themselves beautiful for Benny's birthday. Benny sings while washing himself in the tub. "I can't wait to see my presents," he says.

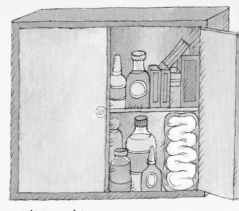

medicine cabinet

lamp

faucet

sponge

shower

bathtub

duckie

mirror

sink

soap

bath mat

washcloth

towel

shampoo

bubble bath

toothbrush

brush

combs

toothpaste

86

wardrobe closet

toilet

toilet paper

slippers

clothes hanger

bow tie

tie

bow

dress

jacket

chair

shoes

"And I can't wait to see who will win Daddy's contest!" says Ophelia with a giggle. It's clear she already believes she's the winner. Her brother looks at her and giggles, too. Then Ophelia and Horatio hum a harmonious melody: "*Ding-ding, ding, ding, ding, ding-ding!*" What can it mean? Let's not waste time. Turn the page and see the end of this mystery.

THE MYSTERY SOLVED

Here we are at Benny's birthday. All the guests are bringing the presents. The first is from Mommy Merry, who offers Benny the "do-it-yourself" kit. "Oh, thanks!" exclaims Benny. "There's even a three-square file, also called a triangular file. Now I can really dedicate myself to my carpentry work!" Does this mean Mommy Merry has won the contest? Daddy Felicity indicates no by shaking his head.

Here come Megan and Marky, who give Benny a picture. "I drew birds flying in a triangular formation, and my sister painted it," says Marky. "Thank you so much!" exclaims Benny. "Now my room will be perfect!" Have the two little Merrys won the contest? No, says Daddy Felicity, shaking his head again.

Now it's the Allegro family's turn. Hillary says, "We decided to give you a telescope with which you can study the stars." Mommy Allegro accompanies Hillary's words with a few harmonious notes on the bagpipe, and little Isidore adds the ringing of a bell. "Thanks to all of you," smiles Benny. "Now I can finally examine the Triangle constellation!" Everyone is ready to congratulate the Allegros, but Daddy Felicity shakes his head in another silent no.

The Felicity grandparents give their grandson an electronic keyboard. Then Horatio and Ophelia give their little brother a music box. But they aren't the winners either. Who's still missing?

Benny Felicity

Daddy and Mommy Felicity

triangular file

Mommy Merry

bird painting

Megan and Marky Merry

"do-it-yourself" kit

telescope

Captain Allegro

bagpipe

Mommy Allegro

Hillary Allegro

bell

Isidore Allegro

electronic keyboard

Felicity grandparents

music box

Horatio and Ophelia Felicity

AND THE WINNER IS—

Ding-ding-ding! comes a sound from behind Benny.
Entering the room is Daddy Merry, and with a small
metal rod he plays on a metal triangle.
"Here's my present!" he exclaims.
"Oh! How did you ever guess what I wanted
most of all?" asks Benny.

musical
triangle

Daddy
Merry

festoon

lamp

cap

glass

pudding

candies

fruit cake

knife

orange soda

dessert fork

dessert knife

plate

fork

spoon

There are no more doubts: the winner is Daddy Merry, and the mysterious gift is the musical instrument known as a triangle.
Everyone applauds, and Daddy Felicity, creator of the contest, is the one who applauds the most. What a party! Everyone is laughing and excited and happy.

glass

candles

pie

birthday cake

fruit

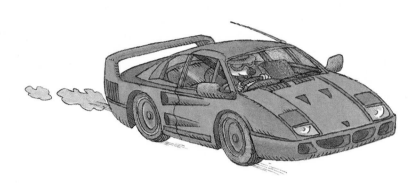

THE WORDS OF

accordion	boarding	castle	cook	duck	foot soldier	herring	light
airplane	boat	catfish	coral	duckie	fork	hoe	lighthouse
aisle	book	cattail	corn	dump	forklift	hold	lightship
algae	bookstore	cave	cotton candy	Earth	fortune-teller	honeysuckle	lilac
aloe	booth	cello	counter	eel	fountain	hook	lily
ambulance	bottle	cement	cow	egg	fountain pen	hook-and-ladder truck	line
anchor	bouquet	chair	crab	eggplant	foxglove	horn	linen
anemone	bow tie	chalk	crane	electric	freight train	horse	living room
antenna	box	change	crate	electrician	French fry	hose	lobster
apple	bread	chart	cream	electric guitar	frog	hot-air balloon	locomotive
armor	brick	check-out counter	crossing	electronic	fruit	housewares	lodge
arrival	bridge	cheese	cruise ship	elevator	frying pan	ice cream	lollipop
astronaut	brush	chestnut	cuckoo	engine	furrow	India ink	loose-leaf book
attendant	bubble	chick	cucumber	entrance	garage	inlet	luggage
baby	bud	chicken	cup	envelopes	gardener	island	lunar vehicle
bag	bulldozer	chicken coop	customs	eraser	gas	ivy	maid
baggage	bunk	children	cutter	escalator	gate	jacket	mailbox
bagpipe	buoy	chimney	cymbals	fairy tale	glass	jasmine	mannequin
bakery	bus	chocolate	dahlia	fallen leaves	glider	jellyfish	map
ball	butter	chrysanthemum	daisy	faucet	glove	jet plane	margarine
balloon	butterfly	church	dance	fax	glue	jogging	marker
banana	cabin	circle	deck	fern	goat	juice	Mars
banner	cabinet	city	delivery	Ferris wheel	goods	jump	mask
barber	cable	clarinet	department	ferry boat	goose	Jupiter	mason
barge	cactus	clerk	departure	festoon	grape	kettledrum	mast
barometer	cake	clock	desk	fife	grapefruit	key	master
basket	calculator	closet	dessert	file	grass	keyboard	mat
bass	calendar	clothes hook	detergent	fir	guitar	king	measure
bass drum	candle	clothing	directory	fireboat	gulf	kingfisher	measuring cup
bassoon	candy	cloud	display	fire extinguisher	hall	kitchen	meat
bathroom	canned goods	clown	diver	firefighter	ham	kite	mechanic
bath tub	cap	coal	dock	fireplace	hammer	knife	medicine
battlement	capsize	coast	dog rose	fish	hangar	knight	melon
beach	car	coast guard	"do-it-yourself" kit	fishing boat	hanger	ladder	menu
bed	card	cockpit	doll	fishing line	harbor	ladle	merchant ship
bedroom	caretaker	cod	dolphin	fishing net	harmonica	lake	Mercury
bee	carnation	coffee	dough	fishing pole	harp	lamp	merry-go-round
bell	carp	collector	dove	flap	hat	lance	meteorite
bench	carpenter	comb	dragonfly	flipper	hay loft	landing	milk
bicycle	carriage	compact disk	drain	float	hazelnut	leaves	mill
binoculars	carrier	compass	drawbridge	florist	headphones	lemon	mimosa
bird	carrot	computer	dress	flour	hedge	letter	mineral water
birthday	cart	conductor	drill	flower	hedgehog	lettuce	minstrel
blackbird	case	constellation	driver	flute	helicopter	library	mirror
blackboard	cashier	container	drum	flying fish	helmethen	lifeguard	mixer
block	cassette	control	drummer		hermit crab	lift	model

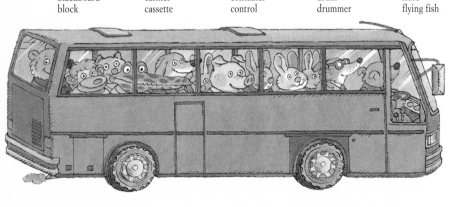

MY FIRST BOOK

monkey bars	pants	pop-up book	rock	shampoo	stake	telescope	turnip
monument	paper	porch	rocking chair	shark	stall	television	turtle
moon	paper clip	portable	roller coaster	sheep	stand	tender	typewriter
moray eel	parachute	porter	roller skates	sheet	stapler	theater	umbrella
moss	parachutist	post	rolling pin	sheet music	star	thermometer	Uranus
motor	parking	poster	roof	shell	starfish	throne	valley
motorboat	passageway	pot	room	ship	station	ticket	van
motorcycle	passenger	potato	rooster	shoe	steam	tie	vehicle
motorized raft	path	primrose	rope	shop	stepping-stone	tile	Venus
mountain	patio	printer	rose	shopper	stern	toad	video
movie	pear	probe	rudder	shopping cart	stewardess	toilet	vinegar
museum	pebble	promontory	ruler	shovel	stone	token	violet
mushroom	pedestrian	propeller	runway	shower	stool	tomato	violin
music box	pen	prow	sail	shrimp	stop	tool	wagon
mussel	pencil	pudding	sailboat	shuttle	store	toothbrush	wait
mustard	pencil sharpener	pump	sailor	sidewalk	stove	toothpaste	waitress
napkin	pepper	pumper truck	salad	signal	strainer	top	wall
nautical	perch	purse	salami	sink	strawberry	tourist	wardrobe
Neptune	perfume	queen	sales clerk	siren	stream	towel	warehouse
nest	pharmacy	rabbit	salt	skateboard	street	tower	wash
net	photocopier	race	sand	skate	string	tow truck	washcloth
newspaper	piano	radar	sardine	ski	string bean	toy	wastebasket
nightingale	pie	radiator	satellite	skirt	submarine	tracks	water
notebook	pig	radio	Saturn	sled	subway	tractor	watercolors
notepad	pigeon	raft	sausage	slide	succulent	traffic	waterfall
oar	pike	rail	saw	slipper	sugar	trailer	watering can
observation deck	pillow	rain	sawfish	slope	suit	train	waterlily
octopus	pilothouse	raincoat	saxophone	smokestack	suitcase	trap	watermelon
office	pincers	rake	scale	snail	sun	traveler	wave
officer	pine	ramp	schedule	snake	swallow	tree	weeping willow
oil	pineapple	raspberries	school	snow	swan	triangle	whale
operator	pitchfork	ray	scissors	snowman	sweater	triangular	wharf
orange	plane	record	scooter	soap	swing	trolley	wheelbarrow
orchestra	plasterer	recorder	screwdriver	soda	swordfish	trombone	whortleberry
orchid	plate	record player	scuba	sole	table	trout	window
oven	platform	rectangle	sea	space	tack	truck	wind surfer
oyster	player	reef	seagull	spaceship	tadpole	trumpet	wing
page	pliers	refrigerator	seahorse	spaghetti	take-off	trumpeters	wood
pail	plum	restaurant	seal	sparrow	tale	trunk	worker
paint	plumber	rhombus	seaplane	speaker	tambourine	try-on room	wrench
painter	plumbing	rice	sea snail	sponge	tanker	T-shirt	xylophone
painting	Pluto	ring-around-the-rosy	seat	spoon	tape	tuba	yacht
pallet	pneumatic	river	seed	square	taxi	tulip	yard
palm	pole	road	sentry	squash	teacher	tuna	yogurt
pan	police	roast	service	squid	teapot	tunnel	zinnia
pansy	pond	robin	set	stairs	telephone	turkey